CLARINET

50 POP SONGS
FOR KIDS

Available for
FLUTE, OBOE, CLARINET, ALTO SAX, TENOR SAX, TRUMPET, HORN,
TROMBONE, VIOLIN, VIOLA, CELLO, RECORDER, and MALLET PERCUSSION

ISBN 978-1-70510-735-5

Visit Hal Leonard Online at
www.halleonard.com

Contact us:
Hal Leonard
7777 West Bluemound Road
Milwaukee, WI 53213
Email: info@halleonard.com

In Europe, contact:
Hal Leonard Europe Limited
42 Wigmore Street
Marylebone, London, W1U 2RN
Email: info@halleonardeurope.com

In Australia, contact:
Hal Leonard Australia Pty. Ltd.
4 Lentara Court
Cheltenham, Victoria, 3192 Australia
Email: info@halleonard.com.au

ANOTHER ONE BITES THE DUST

CLARINET

Words and Music by
JOHN DEACON

BELIEVER

Clarinet

Words and Music by DAN REYNOLDS,
WAYNE SERMON, BEN McKEE, DANIEL PLATZMAN,
JUSTIN TRANTOR, MATTIAS LARSSON and ROBIN FREDRICKSSON

CALL ME MAYBE

CLARINET

Words and Music by CARLY RAE JEPSEN,
JOSHUA RAMSAY and TAVISH CROWE

To Coda

D.S. al Coda
(no repeat)

CODA

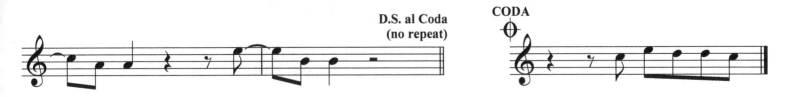

CAN'T STOP THE FEELING!

from TROLLS

CLARINET

Words and Music by JUSTIN TIMBERLAKE,
MAX MARTIN and SHELLBACK

EVERYTHING IS AWESOME
(Awesome Remixx!!!)
from THE LEGO MOVIE

Clarinet

Words by SHAWN PATTERSON
Music by ANDREW SAMBERG,
JORMA TACCONE, AKIVA SCHAFFER,
JOSHUA BARTHOLOMEW, LISA HARRITON
and SHAWN PATTERSON

DANCE MONKEY

CLARINET

Words and Music by
TONI WATSON

DON'T FEAR THE REAPER

CLARINET

Words and Music by
DONALD ROESER

DON'T STOP BELIEVIN'

CLARINET

Words and Music by STEVE PERRY,
NEAL SCHON and JONATHAN CAIN

Moderate Rock

14

FEEL IT STILL

Clarinet

Words and Music by JOHN GOURLEY,
ZACH CAROTHERS, JASON SECHRIST, ERIC HOWK,
KYLE O'QUIN, BRIAN HOLLAND, FREDDIE GORMAN,
GEORGIA DOBBINS, ROBERT BATEMAN, WILLIAM GARRETT,
JOHN HILL and ASA TACCONE

FIGHT SONG

CLARINET

Words and Music by RACHEL PLATTEN
and DAVE BASSETT

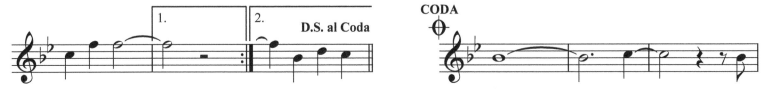

17

FOREVER YOUNG

Clarinet

Words and Music by ROD STEWART,
KEVIN SAVIGAR, JIM CREGAN
and BOB DYLAN

FREE FALLIN'

CLARINET

Words and Music by TOM PETTY
and JEFF LYNNE

HALLELUJAH

CLARINET

Words and Music by
LEONARD COHEN

HAPPY
from DESPICABLE ME 2

Clarinet

Words and Music by
PHARRELL WILLIAMS

Moderately fast

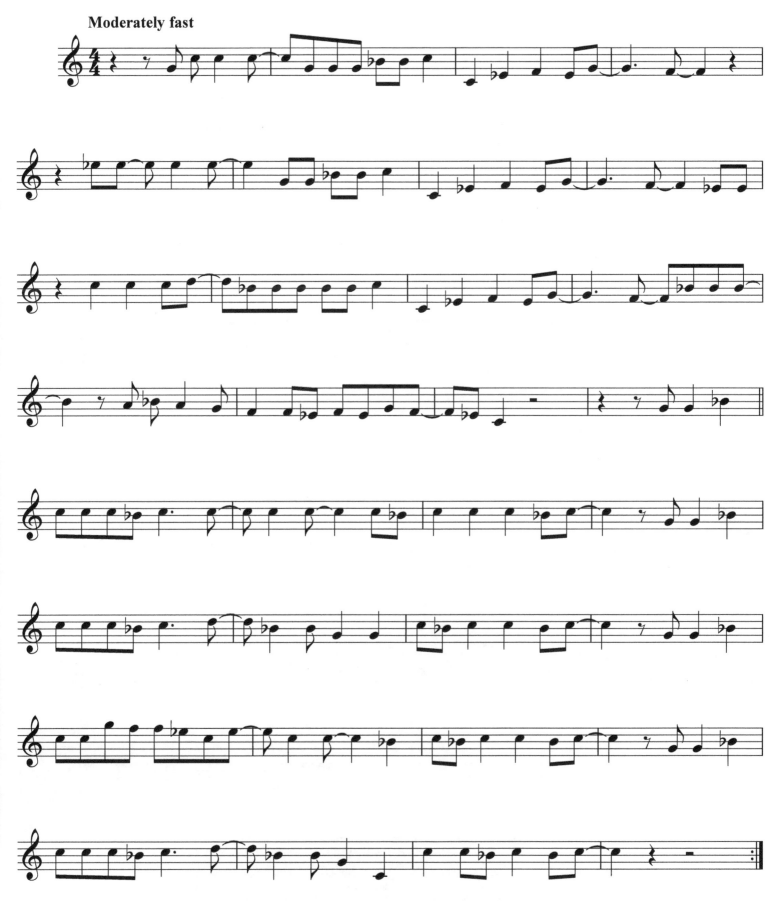

HIGH HOPES

CLARINET

Words and Music by BRENDON URIE,
SAMUEL HOLLANDER, WILLIAM LOBBAN BEAN,
JONAS JEBERG, JACOB SINCLAIR,
JENNY OWEN YOUNGS, ILSEY JUBER,
LAUREN PRITCHARD and TAYLA PARX

To Coda

D.S. al Coda

CODA

HOUND DOG

CLARINET

Words and Music by JERRY LEIBER
and MIKE STOLLER

LOUIE, LOUIE

CLARINET

Words and Music by
RICHARD BERRY

I DON'T CARE

CLARINET

Words and Music by ED SHEERAN,
JUSTIN BIEBER, FRED GIBSON,
JASON BOYD, MAX MARTIN
and SHELLBACK

Syncopated Pop

IN THE AIR TONIGHT

CLARINET

Words and Music by
PHIL COLLINS

Fine

D.S. al Fine

INTO THE GROOVE

CLARINET

Words and Music by STEPHEN BRAY
and MADONNA CICCONE

INTO THE UNKNOWN
from FROZEN 2

Clarinet

Music and Lyrics by KRISTEN ANDERSON-LOPEZ
and ROBERT LOPEZ

Mysteriously, in 2

LET IT BE

CLARINET

Words and Music by JOHN LENNON
PAUL McCARTNEY

To Coda ⊕

D.S. al Coda

CODA
⊕

LET'S GET IT STARTED

CLARINET

Words and Music by WILL ADAMS,
ALLAN PINEDA, JAIME GOMEZ,
MICHAEL FRATANTUNO, GEORGE PAJON JR.
and TERENCE YOSHIAKI GRAVES

THE MIDDLE

Clarinet

Words and Music by SARAH AARONS,
MARCUS LOMAX, JORDAN JOHNSON,
ANTON ZASLAVSKI, KYLE TREWARTHA,
MICHAEL TREWARTHA and STEFAN JOHNSON

A MILLION DREAMS

from THE GREATEST SHOWMAN

CLARINET

Words and Music by BENJ PASEK
and JUSTIN PAUL

NO TEARS LEFT TO CRY

CLARINET

Words and Music by ARIANA GRANDE,
SAVAN KOTECHA, MAX MARTIN
and ILYA

OCEAN EYES

CLARINET

Words and Music by
FINNEAS O'CONNELL

PERFECT

CLARINET

Words and Music by
ED SHEERAN

OLD TOWN ROAD
(Remix)

CLARINET

Words and Music by TRENT REZNOR,
BILLY RAY CYRUS, JOCELYN DONALD,
ATTICUS ROSS, KIOWA ROUKEMA
and MONTERO LAMAR HILL

PARTY IN THE U.S.A.

CLARINET

Words and Music by JESSICA CORNISH,
LUKASZ GOTTWALD and CLAUDE KELLY

PROUD MARY

CLARINET

Words and Music by
JOHN FOGERTY

RESPECT

CLARINET

Words and Music by
OTIS REDDING

REWRITE THE STARS

from THE GREATEST SHOWMAN

CLARINET

Words and Music by BENJ PASEK
and JUSTIN PAUL

SPIRIT
from THE LION KING 2019

CLARINET

Written by TIMOTHY McKENZIE,
ILYA SALMANZADEH and BEYONCÉ

SCARS TO YOUR BEAUTIFUL

CLARINET

Words and Music by ALESSIA CARACCIOLO,
WARREN FELDER, COLERIDGE TILLMAN
and ANDREW WANSEL

SUCKER

CLARINET

Words and Music by NICK JONAS,
JOSEPH JONAS, MILES ALE,
MUSTAFA AHMED, RYAN TEDDER,
LOUIS BELL, ADAM FEENEY,
KEVIN JONAS and HOMER STEINWEISS

Upbeat Pop

SURFIN' U.S.A.

CLARINET

Words and Music by
CHUCK BERRY

SWEET HOME ALABAMA

CLARINET

Words and Music by RONNIE VAN ZANT,
ED KING and GARY ROSSINGTON

TOMORROW
from the Musical Production ANNIE

CLARINET

Lyric by MARTIN CHARNIN
Music by CHARLES STROUSE

A THOUSAND MILES

CLARINET

Words and Music by
VANESSA CARLTON

TWIST AND SHOUT

Clarinet

Words and Music by BERT RUSSELL
and PHIL MEDLEY

WE WILL ROCK YOU

CLARINET

Words and Music by
BRIAN MAY

VIVA LA VIDA

CLARINET

Words and Music by GUY BERRYMAN,
JON BUCKLAND, WILL CHAMPION
and CHRIS MARTIN

WE ARE NEVER EVER GETTING BACK TOGETHER

CLARINET

Words and Music by TAYLOR SWIFT, MAX MARTIN and SHELLBACK

To Coda $\oplus$

1.

2.

D.S. al Coda

CODA $\oplus$

WHAT ABOUT US

CLARINET

Words and Music by ALECIA MOORE,
STEVE MAC and JOHNNY McDAID

WISH YOU WERE HERE

CLARINET

Words and Music by ROGER WATERS
and DAVID GILMOUR

WHATEVER IT TAKES

CLARINET

Words and Music by DAN REYNOLDS,
WAYNE SERMON, BEN McKEE,
DANIEL PLATZMAN and JOEL LITTLE

Y.M.C.A.

CLARINET

Words and Music by JACQUES MORALI,
HENRI BELOLO and VICTOR WILLIS

YOU CAN CALL ME AL

CLARINET

Words and Music by
PAUL SIMON

YOU WILL BE FOUND

from DEAR EVAN HANSEN

CLARINET

Music and Lyrics by BENJ PASEK
and JUSTIN PAUL